Balsamic Reductions

by
Anneke Schoneveld

About the Author

Anneke Schoneveld is a Brooklyn-based food writer and photographer. Working her way through college as a chef, Schoneveld earned her degree in photography and entrepreneurial business/marketing from Virginia Commonwealth University. Moving from restaurant kitchens to the film industry, Schoneveld has become an award-winning commercial director focusing on food marketing and advertising. This is her first cookbook.

Special Thanks

Though this book is dedicated first and foremost to my kickstarter project supporters, there are some people without whom this book would not have made it to the finish line. To my mother: you are an inspiration. You gave me the gift of creativity with no boundaries and without you on the other end of those countless phone calls I doubt I could have finished anything. To my father: you taught me to dream bigger than my life and see potential in everything, and without you doing the dishes I may never have learned to cook. To my Ome David: you let me bring everyone of these photos to life. Your generosity has been life-changing and I will never forget how you saved me.

Carolyn Edgecomb - thank you for all your design help, all of these pages look better because of you. Pamler Enfield - your support has been epic. Thank you for helping me find my focus. David Nicholas - your generosity and talent have given me strength through out so many projects. I want you to know that I'm forever grateful for the opportunity to work with you.

With a special dedication to my niece Elena Sage who is strong and brave.

And to Jonathan David for whom everything in my life is dedicated.

Balsamic Reductions 2011. Copyright © 2011 by Anneke Schoneveld. All rights reserved. Printed in the USA. No part of this book may be used or reproduced in any manner without written permission except in the case of brief quotations embodied in critical articles and reviews. For more information send contact inquiries through:

www.balsamicreductions.com

All photography & text by Anneke Schoneveld 2011

Design & Layout by Anneke Schoneveld with special thanks to Carolyn Edgecomb

Copyedited by Rachel Salowitz

I am exhausted. I am drained. This past year has been hard for a lot of people: the economy has been in the dumps, jobs have been lost, raises have disappeared. New York to begin again. By the time I arrived here I felt weak and brittle, like my bones had been drained of marrow.

...When I taste something sharp with vinegar it's like a magic potion. I feel alive again, even if only on my tongue. Clinging to that part of me that feels life, I have fallen in love with the hot pickled vegetables that Bklyn Larder puts on their salami and provolone sandwich.

I have decided to spend this year nourishing myself, quite literally, back to a spiritual balance. I am going to feed myself healthy again, so I am investing in what makes me feel alive. I am going to write about what I find that is inspiring enough to my palate to bring me back to life.

-Balsamic Reductions post 03/2010

This is how this project began, nearly two years ago, but this is not where it ended. You are holding this book in your hands because of the amazing adventure that my blog started in my life and the people who came out to support me along the way. I am dedicating this book to those people, the people who supported my dreams and knew I was destined to be strong again.

1

CRAVINGS

> "One cannot think well, love well, sleep well, if one has not dined well."
>
> —Virginia Woolf

> "How do they taste? They taste like more."
>
> — H.L. Mencken

I grew up in the west with a lemon tree growing in my backyard. Cravings, for me, aren't forbidden foods. They are the fruition of those farmer's market inspirations, the jewelry of the dinner plate, and a chance to make your meal extraordinary. Vegetables were never meant to be boring. They are crave-worthy. When they're done right, they taste like more.

In classic romantic comedy style, I didn't even like them when I first met them. They had such potential to be loved, but fell flat of any of the excitement that their name built them up to be. What's not to love about stuffed jalapeños? At the beginning of this story – plenty.

I had just moved to the East Coast and was being introduced to the wonderful world of fried snack foods. They sounded sexy, starting with a scooped-out shell of loveliness, filled to the brim with cheese, then breaded and fried. I'm not normally ever against something being filled to oozing with melting cheese, so I should have fallen in love right there, but something had happened to those jalapeños that I wasn't prepared for. They were so filled with cream cheese they had no kick left to them and were fried so dark brown they had no texture of their own to stand on. I love jalapeños for what they are – spicy bites of happiness. Mine is a true love and enough cream cheese can take take the spice out of anything. This love story was not heading in the right direction.

This was only Act 1 and the hero is never ready for victory in Act 1. As with every good love story my champions were destined to overcome and win my heart, but it was a good ten years before I let them back in my life.

I had been ignoring these disappointing flavorless versions of eating peppers (I can barely buy hot salsa in these parts – what's with the obsession with mild?), but all that changed just a few weeks ago. An old roommate set out to make some jalapeños. She blended some cheddar into the filling and had had such failure at frying that she baked them instead. My interest was piqued (as real cheese will always do).

Cheddar? They could be baked? I'd never seen someone make them at home before… maybe they could be inspiring after all.

The pile of jalapeños I bought were sitting on the counter looking so tempting and flavorful. How could something so beautiful and full of potential have gone so wrong? Maybe they had just been mistreated or lead astray. Maybe they deserved a real chance.

A love like this deserves only what is good and none of what went wrong. I dropped cream cheese from the recipe altogether. Why not treat them more like stuffed peppers than the fried snacks everyone thought of them as? My filling blend started to get interesting. Cilantro, fresh corn, tomato, red onion in a minuscule dice… hell, I'd throw caution to the wind! If this could really be love I'd go all in. Bacon is the love potion that can turn any story around.

I mixed everything together and fill all 20 of my jalapeño boats. Topped with cheddar to let them be as pretty as they deserve to be, I put them in the oven to work out their magic.

There's always a scene in every romantic comedy when the characters finally realize that they are made for each other despite their former fighting and tension. We already know it's coming. We saw the stars on the poster together. We know they will fall in love, it's just a matter of watching how it happens. We just hope that the scene is written well enough that we can endure the potential cheesiness of the reveal.

Well this story is no different. A girl like me was never meant to be without this passion. Jalapeños with bacon, cilantro and real cheese? I never had a chance. I was just waiting for them to live up to their potential. Jalapeños actually taste like a vegetable. They still have some spice left to them but are filled with flavor and texture. They still ooze (no one ever wanted them to lose that precious quality), but now they string out cheese between crisp pops of fresh summery corn and salty bites of bacon. Now I really am ready to go off and watch my sunset with my spicy bites of happiness.

STUFFED JALAPEÑOS

14 - 16 jalapeño peppers*

7 strips cooked bacon (chopped)

1/4 cup red onion (tiny dice)

1/3 cup chopped fresh cilantro

1/4 cup diced tomato (tiny dice – discarding the seeds)

1 ear fresh corn

1/2 cup shredded jack cheese

salt + pepper (to taste)

1 tsp garlic powder

cheddar cheese to top the filled peppers

The Madness

Preheat the oven to 375°.

Slice the jalapeños in half lengthwise and scrape out the seeds and ribs from each jalapeño with a small paring knife. Mix together all the filling ingredients except the cheddar cheese. Fill each pepper half with the mix and top with a slice of cheddar cheese. Arrange the peppers on a foil-lined baking sheet and bake for 20-30 minutes, or until the cheese is bubbly and lightly browned and the peppers are cooked. Allow to cool for 5 minutes before serving.

Makes 28-32 servings*

The Warning

*I know that this is a potentially excessive amount of jalapenos. I always tend to make too much food. You can actually sit and eat a pile of these – they're like tortilla-free quesadillas and a gluten-free meal.

THE ULTIMATE LEMONADE

3/4 cup sugar

3/4 cup water (for simple syrup)

1 cup lemon juice

3 - 4 cups cold soda water

The Madness

Heat your water in a small saucepan and add the sugar. Stir until the sugar dissolves completely. Set aside to cool.

If you're really making the ultimate lemonade you'll want to juice 4 to 6 lemons, enough for one cup of juice.

Add the juice and the sugar water to a pitcher. Add 3 to 4 cups of cold soda water to the desired strength. Refrigerate 30 to 40 minutes. If the lemonade is a little sweet for your taste, add a little more straight lemon juice to it. Serve with ice and sliced lemons.

CORN SALSA

1 ripe avocado (diced)

1 cup cherry tomatoes (quartered)

2 ears fresh corn

1/2 cup red onion (diced fine)

2 jalapeños (seeded + diced)

2 - 3 tbsp fresh lime juice

1/2 cup chopped fresh cilantro

sea salt + pepper (to taste)

The Madness

Pile veggies into a medium mixing bowl. Hold the corn over the bowl and cut off the kernels half a cob at a time (bottom half, flip, then the other half) for less mess.

In a small bowl mix your lime juice, sea salt, cilantro and fresh black pepper. Dress your veggies with the mixture and serve.

Summer Lovin'

Ah summer. Season of beauty and heat. Time of refreshing and extra vitamin D. How I love you.

I love you for bringing us all outside to explore the world like winter never could. I fall for you even more when I step out of my door and discover a street fair happening just beyond the world of my desk. My passion for you grows deeper still when I realize you love me enough to bring out the corn-on-the-cob guy.

If you ever thought the simple beauty of fresh corn was complete with just a little butter and salt, then you need to meet the street fair corn-on-the-cob guy. My mother taught me nature has done all the work to make food taste amazing - your only goal is to not mess it up - but I now know that there can be even more. Though corn on the cob is nearly summer perfection eaten plain and so lightly steamed that it's almost raw, my street fair master has made it an art, grilled to a beautiful smoky char over low heat coals. He knows to keep a great arm of stalk to hold onto while you eat, because you're gonna make a mess of yourself otherwise when you add dripping levels of jalapeño-honey butter, a dusting of chili pepper, and a bright squeeze of lime.

Ah summer – beautiful and sweet. So sweet that its bounty cannot be summed up with just a dish that brings us back to our childhood by letting us eat with our hands. That's why the corn-on-the-cob guy can never be set up very far from the siren's song of the fresh lemonade guy.

Nothing goes with summer like fresh lemonade, ice cold and tart yet sweet on a hot day. Ah summer – how I love you.

I can't stay away from my desk all day, so I save the best for last and take it home with me. You can smell it from a block away, true masters at work and a large meat smoker of pork barbecue and beef brisket. Summer's food pairing of the gods: slow cooked meats with fast cooked veggies all done over fire.

I'm so excited to chat about barbeque that the smoker king actually hands me a big bite of brisket, putting the meat right in my hand. It drips to my elbow almost instantly. It is like heaven to taste the smoke and char melding into the spices and juice of that tender meat. I chose the brisket sandwich, still hot from its charcoal casket, with a dash of barbecue sauce. The foil-wrapped gift they hand me is heavy and warm. It must be good to live in Australia where summer and Christmas go hand in hand, 'cause this is the kind of presents you could get.

I do manage to get back to my work, but I can't focus on anything until the last savory bite is gone. Even then I'm in a bit of a euphoria. Maybe if I can focus and get my work done before dark there will still be a funnel cake guy outside and I can re-live falling in love with summertime all over again.

a debate in breakfast

> Santana: Breakfast confuses you.
>
> Brittany: Sometimes it's sweet, sometimes it's salty. What if I have eggs for dinner? What is that?
>
> —Glee 2011

What if you have pancakes for dinner?!?! What is that? Binner? Breakner? Brinner? ...whatever it is – it's clearly not as catchy as brunch and it doesn't get nearly enough creative attention.

I am a fan of the breakfast-dinner. It's actually traditional for my family to have pancakes for dinner. My father is from Holland and there pancake houses there don't even open for breakfast. Pannekoek, or "Papa's pancakes" as we called them, are Dutch pancakes as thin as crepes and as large as your plate. We rolled them filled with apple sauce and ate them by the dozens. If you had a family as large as mine it starts to make sense that pancakes are too much work for a breakfast time meal.

Pannekoek are so delicious, honestly I'm getting homesick just writing about them.

Not that we never ate pancakes for breakfast. My mom is American and when she busts out a griddle to make traditional Bisquick pancakes, she can churn them out by the millions at a moment's notice. Still, even she's been known to throw them together for an easy dinner.

Who doesn't love pancakes? Well the simple answer is no one. No one doesn't love pancakes. Pancakes, crepes, potato cakes – whatever your fancy, if you fry up a flat cake it's gonna be loved. When I first ran across a recipe for fresh corn cakes I was sure they would be amazing.

Savory, fresh, with juicy bits of corn that pop in your mouth, I think the breakfast dinner has risen to a new stratosphere. I could still serve these with a side of bacon, eggs, even hash brown potatoes, but top it with guacamole and salsa mixed with sour cream. If you can stop yourself from eating too many of them straight from the pan you might even have room for a berry and maple syrup-covered kind of dessert.

fresh corn pancakes

The Method
....
1 large egg • 1 cup milk • 3/4 cup yellow corn meal • 1/2 cup flour • 1 tsp sea salt • 2 tsp baking powder • 1 tsp cayenne pepper • 1/4 cup fresh cilantro • 1/4 cup chopped green onion

The Madness
....
Beat your egg and milk together then throw in your dry ingredients. Mix until you have a batter then add your veggies. Fry them up like normal pancakes in a non-stick frying pan using a nice pat of butter.

*adapted from Sunset magazine

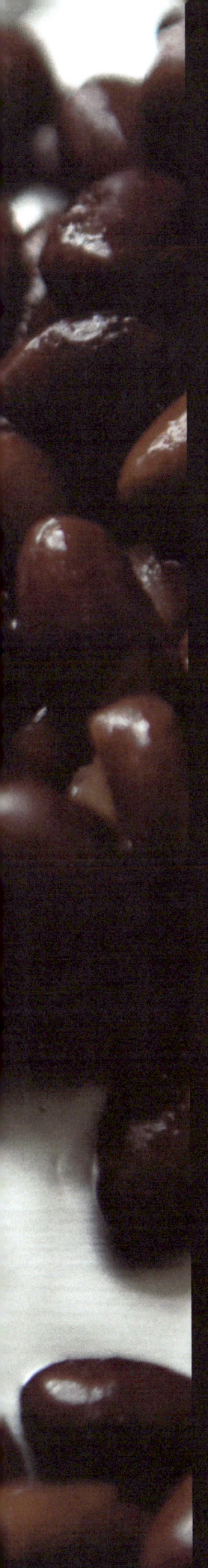

Refried Black Beans

The Method

1 can black beans • 2 tbsp olive oil (+/-) • 1 small onion (diced) • garlic (I like lots, you don't have to) • an (optional) jalapeño • a kick of cayenne pepper

The Madness

Heat your oil in a medium frying pan and sauté your onion until just starting to turn golden. Add your chopped garlic (I'm not kidding, I can use as much as 4-5 cloves when I'm feeling crazy) and jalapeño if you choose to put one in. Give the garlic a minute or two to start sweating and dump in your rinsed beans. Fry for the first time until the beans are heated through. Season with your spices and start to taste. Careful you don't over-salt them as they still need to fry again.

When you're pretty happy with the flavors you've got going on, start smashing your beans with the back of your spoon. Add a half can of water to the pan and stir. Let that fry for the second time as a mash and BAM it's been re-fried. Done. It will still be a bit thin when it needs to come off the heat (the starches will continue to thicken the dish as it cools). Just salt to taste and enjoy! it's really that easy.

Mama's Recipes
Nothing says cravings like your mom's recipes

Mama's Potato Salad

4 lbs small potatoes • 3 large carrots (chopped) • 4 stalks celery (chopped) • 3 hard boiled eggs (chopped) • parsley • 1 green onion • garlic salt (to taste) • 2 tbsp lemon juice • 1/2 tsp salt • 1 tsp mustard • 1 egg (raw) • 1 cup salad oil

The Madness

Cut your potatoes into bite size pieces and boil them in unsalted water until tender. While they are cooking put the lemon juice, salt, mustard and raw egg into the blender with 1/4 cup of salad oil. Blend at a top speed until smooth and thick, then while it's still blending add the remaining oil slowly until you realize it's that easy to make your own mayonnaise.

Drain your potatoes and set them in a large bowl to chill. Blend cool potatoes with your mayo and the remaining ingredients. My mom would top it off with some paprika, more parsley and sliced egg to make it pretty, but that's only for show. Allow the salad to chill for a few hours until ready to serve.

Disclaimer: My mother's recipes come with vague measurements (if any) and funny notes about using the cheapest canned shrimp you can find. I have tried to make these recipes clearer for you, but left my mother's character intact where I could. These recipes are worth trying - even if they seem confusing at times.

CHICKEN IN THE BASKET

A recipe that dates back to my grandmother's generation of cooking from cans, it was my all-time favorite meal to request for my birthday dinner. I love it with lots and lots of extra sauce so I can drown my rice with it. Serve it with rice and a side of green beans.

- **equal parts sour cream, cream of mushroom soup and white wine**
- **enough chicken breasts and thighs to feed your family**

The Madness

Place your chicken in a single layer in a wide baking dish. Mix your sauce together and pour over the chicken. Bake uncovered at 375° for 45 minutes, or until your chicken is fully cooked.

SPANISH RICE

- **2 tbsp olive oil**
- **1 onion (chopped fine)**
- **2 cups white rice**
- **1 lb ground beef**
- **3 cups chicken stock (hot)**
- **1 heaping tbsp tomato paste**
- **1 cup frozen corn (thawed)**
- **salt + pepper**

The Madness

In a large pan brown your rice in olive oil over medium-high heat. Add your onion to the pan stirring frequently, for 4 minutes, until the onions are softened. Add your beef and cook until browned and crumbly.

Microwave your stock until hot and add your remaining ingredients to the rice mixture. Lower heat to medium and simmer for 15-20 minutes until your rice is cooked.

CLAM + SHRIMP SPAGHETTI

- **2 cans chopped clams (save the liquid)**
- **1 can tiny shrimp**
- **2 tsp butter**
- **1 handful parsley (chopped)**
- **1 bunch green onions (chopped)**
- **2 cloves garlic (chopped)**
- **1 3/4 cups clam juice**
- **1/4 cup white wine**
- **1 tbsp cornstarch**
- **a pinch of garlic salt**
- **a few drops of Tabasco**
- **thin spaghetti**

The Madness

This whole thing only takes 20 minutes from start to finish, so get the water boiling for the spaghetti first.

While the spaghetti is cooking, get your butter melting in a large sauce pan. Add the parsley, green onions and some chopped garlic. Let the mixture lightly sauté but don't let it get dark.

In a two-cup measuring cup add the juice from the cans of clams then add clam juice from the bottle to make almost two cups. Add white wine to make two cups. About ¼ cup wine is sufficient.

Add a little garlic salt and a few drops of Tabasco for sparkle. Add the corn starch and mix well.

Add the liquid to the parsley mixture and simmer for about 2 minutes until it thickens (you can add wine to thin it to the consistency you like).

When the spaghetti is cooked and drained, add the clams and shrimp to the sauce, stir, and then add to the spaghetti.

UNCLE GIL'S

This recipe shows up in our house every year after Thanksgiving. It's a great way to use up your leftover turkey and it's tasty made with chicken any time

- **2 cups leftover turkey**
- **1 large onion (sliced)**
- **3 cloves garlic (chopped)**
- **1 tbsp butter**
- **garlic salt**
- **2 cups rice**
- **6 cups turkey broth***
- **white wine**

The Madness

In a large casserole dish break your turkey into bite size pieces and fill the bottom of the dish.

Lightly sauté your onion in butter over medium until it becomes translucent. Add your garlic and cook for 1 minute more. Pour the cooked onion mixture over your turkey.

Pour the rice over the top until you have an even layer. Add your turkey broth. It should cover over all of the rice.

Cover and bake at 350° for 1 hour. Then carefully pull it from the oven and add a bit of white wine (or more broth) over it to moisten, and put it back in to bake uncovered for another 15-20 minutes.

*Save the bones from roast turkeys and chickens and boil them for broth. If you add some carrots, celery, and onion to the bones while they boil you will have an excellent homemade broth to use for soups and Uncle Gil's.

An Adventure in Daal

I once had a vegetarian roommate who I nicknamed "Mango Lassi Man." This is mostly because he painted his room the color of a fluorescent mango. He and I share, a humor-based food relationship. he has been a vegetarian every day of his life, it's rare that he ever even ate eggs, and because if this I loved to enlighten him about the amazing world of carnivores.

It all began just after he moved in. I don't remember what I was cooking, but he asked me the oddest question about bacon. He wanted to know something about when they made bacon. Made bacon? He must have been confused. No no, he went on… when they make bacon. You know, when they take layers of fat and meat and press them together to make bacon. To say I found this amusing would be an understatement. I felt bad that I laughed outright. He was my new roommate – would he be offended that I was laughing at him? Nope. He was so sincere about his question that it never occured to him that it was funny to ask. I explained bacon. He never lived it down. We've both happily discussed the world of meat with fascination ever since.

Having a vegetarian in the house influenced a lot of things about my kitchen. Not only did we keep separate cutting boards and utensils for vegetarian use only, but I now rarely cook meat at home (unless of course it's bacon which is good in just about everything). As much as you'd expect me to be the big cook in the house (and believe me, before he moved in I thought I would be too), every night he was in there methodically making the kitchen smell like spice combinations I found I didn't particularly enjoy.

I traveled to India a few years ago. It is an intensely beautiful and alluring place, full of extremes of every kind. Cows and tuk-tuks fill the street and yellow lights streak through the windows of taxis as complex neighborhoods made of cardboard boxes and metal roofs whiz past. I was bedridden with food poisoning for my first 3 days in the country (if you can't drink the water, don't let your friends feed you seafood). My friend's mother-in-law was worried I would die, but once I was back on my feet I had some of the most glorious and dangerous adventures of my life wandering through the northern regions of the land of mystery.

Other than the realized fear of getting sick, it never occurred to me that a month eating Indian food wouldn't agree with me. Prior to traveling there I think my experience with their cuisine was limited to chicken tikka masala and samosas (potato-stuffed breads). As the only polite way to treat a guest is to keep them

stuffed full of food at all times, a few weeks into my journey I grew tired of the food long before I was ready to leave the culture. So tired, in fact, that it took me over 3 years before I would eat Indian food again. Sadly, that meant I would unfairly not find my roommate's cooking as inspiring as he might have hoped.

He made dal almost every day. The most basic dal is simply cooked lentils. Beans and legumes take a logically starring role in my roommate's diet; the combination of dal and brown rice make a great foundation for him. His dal was smooth and almost soupy, perfect for mixing into your rice, and he generously offered me this goopy, unseasoned mixture to eat. I had only ever tried to make dal once before he moved into my house. To me dal was a spicy lentil dip, the thickness of hummus (which I later discovered was just a northern Indian style of dal). He rarely added seasonings of any kind to his dal as he'd also add spicy vegetables to his meal. For as much as he loved it, I wasn't finding it a very motivating muse.

That was before Auntie arrived. Auntie is my roommate's mother and she arrived in our lives without much fanfare or even preparation on our part. He was having some minor shoulder surgery (which thankfully went very well) and Auntie was coming to look after him while he was laid up for a week. Not only was she the most lovely and sweet houseguest you could ever ask for, but suddenly the kitchen was wafting with romantic, enticing smells of spices and exotic foods. I was enchanted by her and she promised to teach me how to make some of her dishes before the week was out.

She worked her way gracefully through the kitchen as she made dish after dish with no recipe or guide other than her memories and intuition for measurements and taste. She would call me over when it was time to see the next step and take my hand as she explained the process. She was self-conscious when I wanted to photograph the process, but when I assured her I would only show her hands she didn't stop to change into a more formal dress. A spoon of this and a dash of that, each spice being added at its own unique and proper time. She reminded me a bit of a chili master making their secret recipe. It was all so simple but made with such an instinctual, delicate hand. It smelled rustic while it was simple, hearty, and filling, but grew sophisticated and layered with complexity as each step and spice was added.

Even if I could recreate her recipes (which could not be done without copious notes), I think I would still lack her intuition. She made even her most simple dish a creation worth trying. Watching them come together, from simple ingredients with no seasonings in sight to bright and flavorful dishes full of wondrous spice mixes, made me realize that even if I don't want to eat Indian all the time, there is a whole world of inspiration to be found in their unique cuisine and culture.

A sideways glimpse of the Taj Mahal

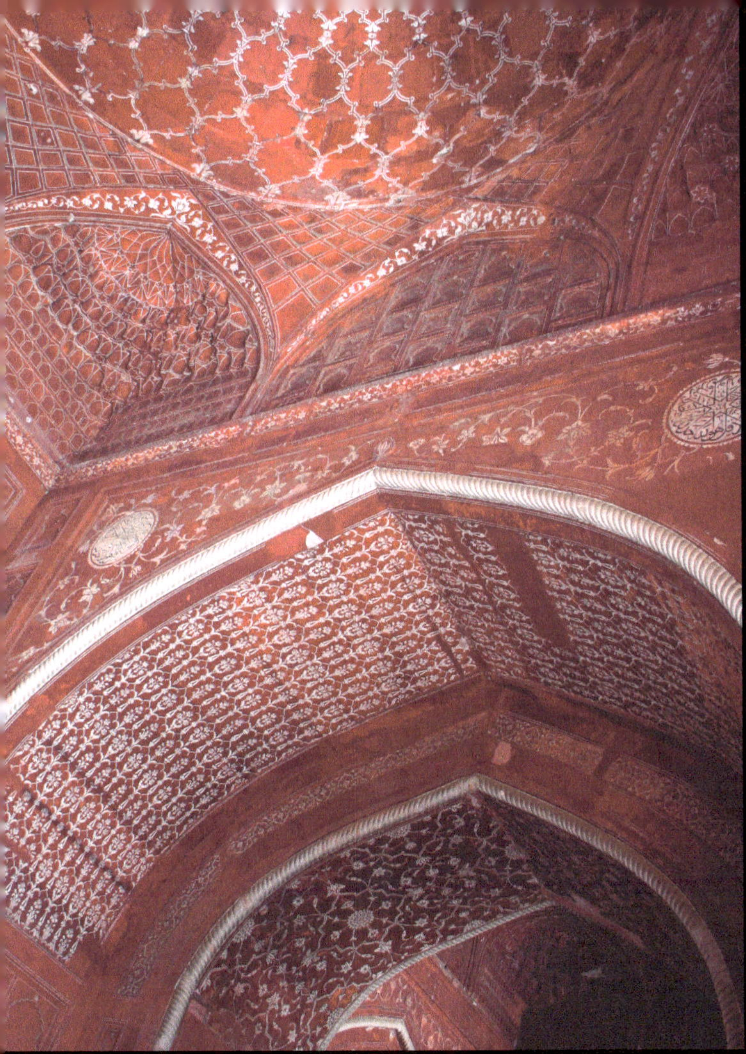

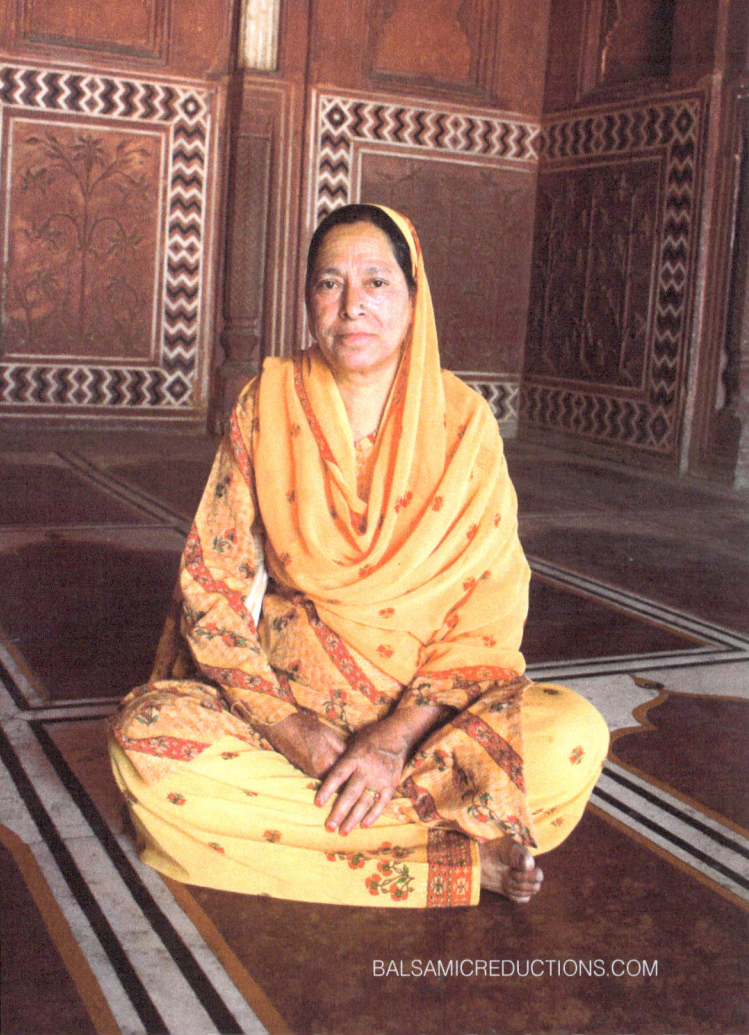

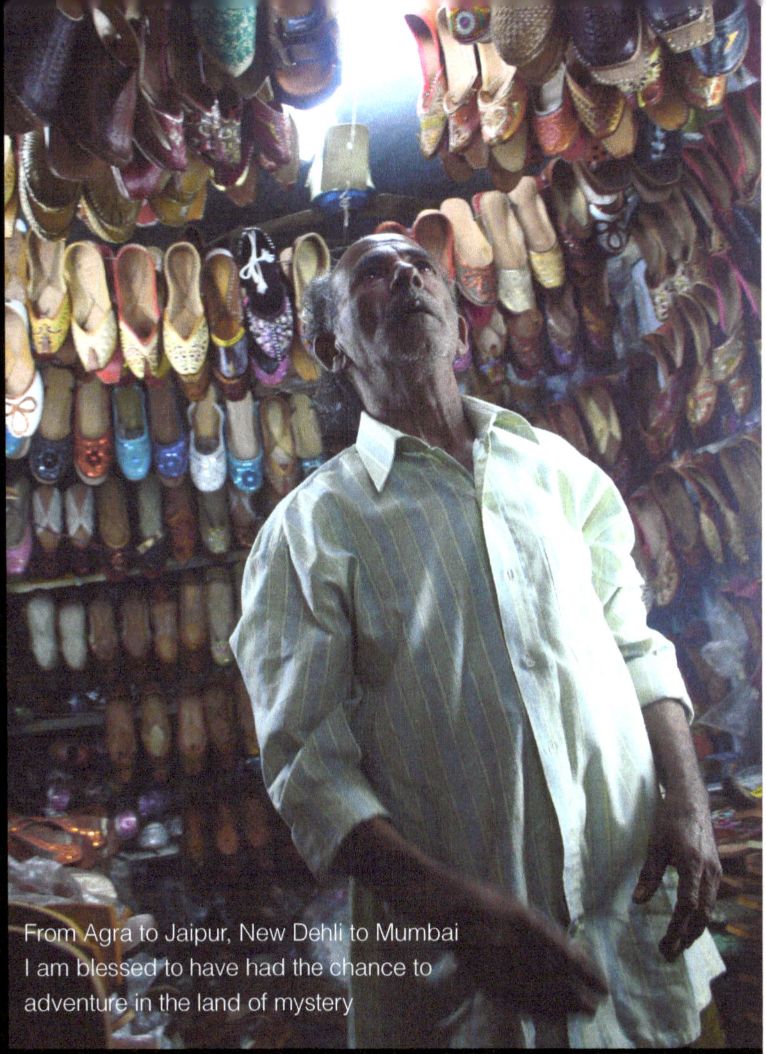
From Agra to Jaipur, New Dehli to Mumbai
I am blessed to have had the chance to
adventure in the land of mystery

PF·
7
4
PF-7
4

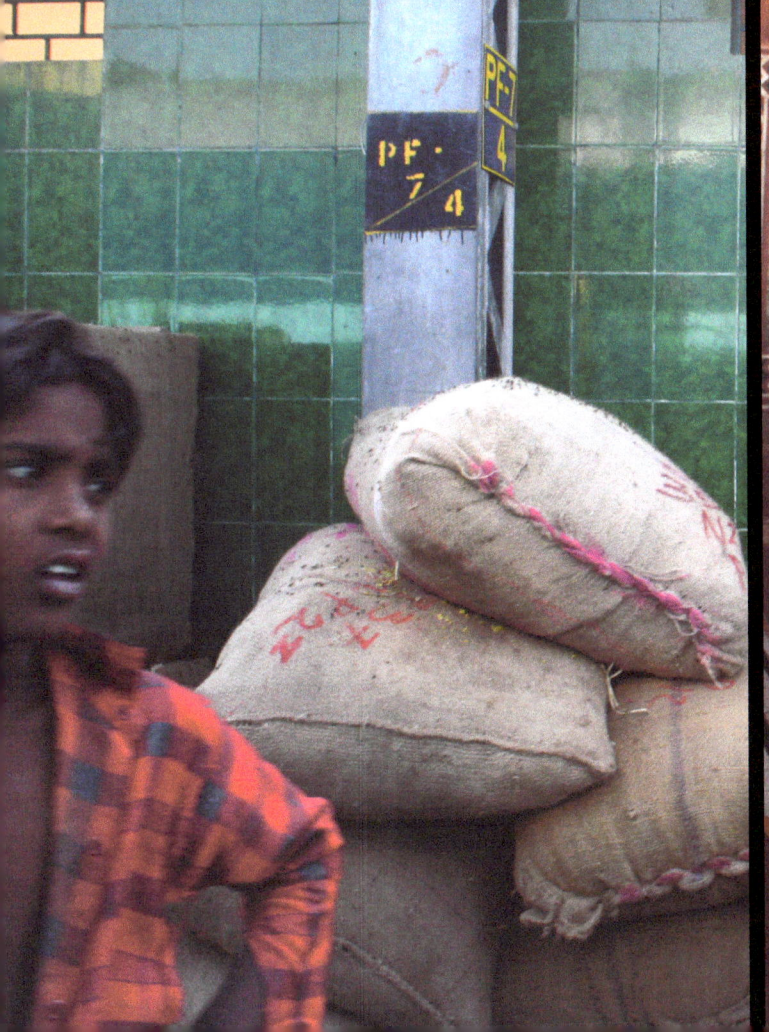

BALSAMICREDUCTIONS.COM

2

DINNER PARTIES

"There is a communication of more than our bodies when bread is broken and wine is drunk. And that is my answer when people ask me: Why do you write about hunger, and not wars or love."

— MFK Fisher

Dinner never really seems complete without filling every seat at the table with people to feed. Coming from a large family I still have trouble scaling down my recipes to feed only a couple of people. Eating together is the beginning of relationship, and feeding people is my favorite way to love them. I will always welcome you over for dinner - especially if your love language is doing the dishes.

Spicy Falafel

The Method

1 can of chickpeas (drained and rinsed)

2 tsp olive oil

1 small red onion (diced small)

1 red bell pepper (diced small)

1 poblano pepper (diced small)

5 cloves of garlic (I like flavorful food if you couldn't tell)

1 tsp cayenne pepper

2 tsp ground cumin

salt & pepper

fresh cilantro

fresh parsley

1 egg

1/3 cup flour (give or take)

canola oil for frying

You want all your veggies diced really quite small to keep the texture of your falafel even. It's a bit more work, but it's totally worth it.

The Madness

Heat your olive oil in a frying pan over medium heat. Add your onions, bell pepper and poblano and sweat them out until the onions are clear but not really browning. Add your garlic cloves crushed and chopped fine. You want all your veggies diced really quite small to keep the texture of your falafel even. It's a bit more work but it's totally worth it.

When your garlic is starting to smell good, add your chickpeas and stir the whole things together. Put in your spices and keep it over the heat until the beans are warm, then turn off the burner while you smash the beans with the back of your spoon. Taste the mixture for salt and spice levels, at this point it should be delicious already. Transfer the mixture to a bowl.

Pile a handful of parsley and cilantro on your cutting board and chop them together. Put about half of this mixture into the bowl with your bean mixture (the rest is for the yogurt sauce) and add your egg. Mix by hand. Start adding flour until it forms a dough consistency. It will still stick to your hands, but that is a small price to pay for the tender texture that these falafel will hold onto with less flour. Put the whole mixture into the fridge to chill.

Heat your canola oil in a clean frying pan at medium heat (I only needed about 1/3 cup). Test the temperature of your oil by dropping a spot of water into it: when it sizzles, you're ready to go.

I like to make small patties from the chilled dough and make more appetizer-sized falafels. You can make them any way you like, but flattened patties work best. After you drop them in the pan check that they move freely and aren't sticking. Flip them when you start to see a golden brown edge forming (about 1-2 minutes). When they're done put them on some paper towels and crack some fresh salt over them. They don't really need more salt – but all fried food is better with a little fresh salt on their fried edges.

Yogurt Sauce

The Method

1 small container of Greek-style plain yogurt • juice of 1 lemon • fresh cilantro • fresh parlsey • salt & pepper

The Madness

Mix together the yogurt, lemon juice and chopped herbs (left over from the above recipe). Then add salt and pepper to taste. Should be a bright, clean flavor. If not, balance it with a little more lemon.

Everyday Cravings

Every party needs an appetizer to keep people at bay while you finish the rest of the food. Or maybe it's just for those days when you need to snack. Hummus is my stand-by. Filling, delicious and incredibly easy to make.

Mama's Hummus

1 can chickpeas (drained but saving the can's liquids) • 2/3 cup liquid from the can of beans • 3 tbsp tahini • 1-2 cloves of garlic • 1/2 tsp sea salt • 2 tbsp olive oil • 2 tsp lemon juice

Put everything into a blender and blend until smooth.

Mama makes all kinds of variations on this - adding sundried tomatoes or roasted red bell pepper. The possibilities are endless so go ahead and have fun.

brunch problem solved

egg cups

The age-old problem is the same for every dinner party, whether at home or in a restaurant kitchen. How do you get all the food done at the same time so people can sit and eat together?

I would say the #1 problem with my first draft dinner party menus is over-scheduling either the oven or stove top. The first thing I'm inspired to make generally leads me to more inspirations that use the same cooking method. If I want to make a roasted veggie platter (and I always do), then the 4 cookie sheets' worth of veggies will take up the oven for the last hour before people arrive. I really need several ovens, but that's not a problem I can solve right now.

Maybe I'm still on a breakfast kick from my waffle dinner party last month, but I got really excited about making egg cups the other day. An egg cup (is that what they're even called or am I being completely uncreative right now?) is like the sunny-side-up cousin to a mini frittata or quiche. I think they look cuter (or at least they can be) and they're even less work than a quiche – which, let's be honest, is a freakishly easy dish to make.

To make an egg cup you simply rub the inside of your dish with butter (I use my herb butter, because if you have a chance to put more flavor into something why wouldn't you?) and line it with ham or prosciutto to form your cup. Then you can start to really get creative with fillings. To finish, crack an egg over top and bake.

Egg cups are the perfect brunch party alternative to making omelets. They're pretty. Everyone can have their own choice of fillings (and they can get as elaborate as you want them to be – which of course I love), and you put them all in the oven at once so everyone can eat at the same time.

Unlike omelets, however, not all fillings are created for equal success in an egg cup. I've found sharper cheeses work better than mild (Parmesan is fantastic in them but requires a little shot of milk/cream to help it blend in with the other flavors). Asparagus is amazing. Tomatoes make them look so much better I can't really imagine leaving them out. A sprig of fresh herbs really shines. Egg cups bake for 15-18 minutes at 350° so herbs have the chance to infuse the dish. I could probably create an infinite number of favorites with this dish. Maybe even a do-it-yourself bar for a brunch party and let people make their own…

Regardless of how delicious and easy these are to make, their biggest advantage for me is that you can quickly bake them just before sitting down to eat. Anything else I may have baked for a brunch would be done before people got there, and my stove-top will probably be taken up with a hash of potatoes or grits or something. These can be served out on a tray with some good bread and you're done: party in minutes!

All fillings are not created equally for success in an egg cup. I've found sharper cheeses work better than mild. Asparagus is amazing. A sprig of fresh herbs really has a chance to shine.

Egg cups bake for 15-18 minutes at 350° so herbs can really have the chance to infuse flavor.

BALSAMICREDUCTIONS.COM

Pistachio Waffles

1 1/2 cups flour • 1/2 cup ground pistachios • 1/3 cup sugar • 1 tbsp baking powder • 1 tsp salt • 2 egg yolks • 1 3/4 cups milk • 1/2 cup melted butter • 2 egg whites

The Madness

In a bowl combine the flour, pistachios, sugar, baking powder and salt. In a second bowl lightly beat the egg yolks. Beat the milk into the yolks first, then add the melted butter into the egg mixture. Pour the egg mixture over the flour mixture and stir until combined but still a bit lumpy. In a metal bowl beat the egg whites until stiff peaks form. Gently fold beaten egg whites into batter. Pour 1 cup batter onto a preheated, lightly greased waffle iron. Bake according to the directions for your waffle iron.

Excuse for a Dinner Party

fresh berry syrup over waffles

If you had an excuse for a dinner party on a Monday, and an excuse to upgrade said party to include several desserts and quite a bit more wine than a weekday generally deserves, there might also be an excuse to invite new friends to the party.

When you're single you can't just ignore Valentine's Day (no matter how much you may want to). All those Facebook posts from your married friends gushing over each other ring a bell to anyone? Not that I'm holding it against them, it's just a darn good annoying example. The thing is, I don't mind Valentine's. For me V-Day is a day to get your single friends together to laugh, eat, drink, and solidify friendships by supporting each other against loneliness. It's the best kind of day for friends, really. So my friends decided the theme for the meal should be bacon, and we would make breakfast for dinner.

I picked up a pint of blueberries and started munching on them while cooking. To my shock, they were the best blueberries I'd ever eaten! Suddenly inspired by their bright, almost citrusy sweetness, I started to make a compote to top our waffles. My mom would just sprinkle a bit of sugar over berries and let them sit until they produced juice. I was sure I could do more to bring out their flavor than just adding sugar. I needed to experiment.

I set a cup of water to boil with a half cup of sugar. I dumped what berries I hadn't already eaten into the pot (about half a pint each of blueberries and chopped strawberries). When it started to make a beautiful purple syrup, I tasted it. It was losing everything that had made those blueberries so irresistible! Strawberries, blueberries, raspberries… their appeal is so much more than their sweetness. It's their bold balance with tartness that makes them worth craving.

No worries, the perfect counterpart to blueberries is lemon. This just needed lemon juice. Somehow I was out of lemon juice (I know – how does that even happen?!!). Horror. I put a whole bunch of lime juice in and set to looking through my cupboards for inspiration.

You can make fun of me later, but to tell you the truth it's one of the most versatile ingredients in my kitchen: I pulled out my bottle of white balsamic vinegar. Brighter and less sweet than its dark counterpart, white balsamic still has that ready-to-drink quality that make the sweeter vinegars sing. I started pouring it in. Not just a splash, mind you - I poured in easily as much vinegar as I did lime juice. A revelation of flavors and balances erupted. Seriously the dessert makers of the world are underestimating vinegars as a source of beauty and inspiration. I was in love.

We told stories and laughed. We made waffles heaven with a bacon crumble and berry syrup. Who would believe that a Monday could be this good?

FRESH BERRY COMPOTE

The Method

- 1 cup water
- 1/2 cup sugar
- 1 tbsp candied orange peels (optional)
- 1 1/2 pints berries (preferably blueberries, but a mix is great too)
- about 1/4 cup lime juice*
- about 1/4 cup white balsamic vinegar*

The Madness

*add these to taste (as I didn't measure while making this) but keeping roughly equal portions of each

Boil the water, sugar and orange peels. Add your berries. When the syrup turns a lovely dark purple add your lime juice and vinegar. Simmer for another 2 minutes and let cool before serving.

BALSAMICREDUCTIONS.COM

"Always start out with a larger pot than what you think you need."
-Julia Child

National Man-Food Day

a.k.a. The Superbowl

I never quite realized how much the Superbowl could mean to me. I mean, I never even know what teams are playing until the game is turned on. I'm more of a connoisseur-of-Superbowl-commercials kind of girl, but with all the food articles and blog postings coming out, like Smitten Kitchen's drool-inducing "if-you're-going-to-do-it-you-might-as-well-go-all-the-way" meatball subs. I was ready to go all in. I called up my guys and invited myself to their house to watch the game.

"Great. Come on over. …but I'm already making dinner and I'm not sure if there will be enough for you…"

"What's for dinner? Baked snapper, wild rice, and broccoli with parsnips."

There was a moment of dead silence on my end of the phone as my head was shocked with this answer. I did a double-take.

What-the-what?!?!

I have never craved man-food more than I did after hearing those words on a Superbowl Sunday. Where are the buffalo wings? The pizza? The nachos? All those amazing foods that will leave that man-food-approved orange grease on my plate?

No worries. I'll bring my own dinner.

I stop at BKLYN Larder and get myself a meatball and provolone sandwich (one of my favorites from their artisan sandwich menu) and a side of macaroni and cheese. The shop is already getting cleaned up for the night, but their guys (and it was all the guys working Superbowl Sunday there – another oddity) stopped everything to get me properly set up to celebrate "National Man-Food Day" (as I was now referring to it). They even gave me a large serving of chili topped with melting cheese and red onion in appreciation of my newly discovered man-food reverence.

As I waited for the subway the bag of food was warm and the wafts of savory temptation maked me excited to be celebrating properly. Even with all this it was still hard, walking past the pizza shops on my way to their apartment, to not stop and buy wings to top off my extravaganza, but let's be honest: for all of my man-food esteem, I'm still just a girl and probably won't even make it through to the chili.

For some people the Superbowl is actually about the football game. I can't really imagine that. For me it's the dude's version of Thanksgiving. It's an excuse to celebrate all the coziness of the rib-sticking foods we otherwise have a hard time allowing ourselves to love as much as we actually want to. It's a time to get together with friends and eat, drink, and be merry. It has all the makings of a national holiday – including being celebrated by most of the nation.

However gratifying it is to see the guys in your life eye your plate of steaming hot man-food while they eat baked fish, there's nothing quite like sharing the love. To my guys – next year I promise I'll host a proper party.

MAC AND CHEESE

- 4 cups macaroni noodles
- 1 egg (beaten)
- 1/4 cup butter
- 1/4 cup flour
- 2 1/2 cups milk (not cold)
- 1 pound extra sharp cheddar cheese (grated)
- 1 tsp salt
- 1 tsp cayenne pepper
- 1/2 tsp pepper
- paprika

The Madness

Preheat your oven to 350° and set your water to boil for your noodles.

Cook your macaroni noodles just until firm. Drain and set aside while you make the sauce. I like to give the noodles a quick cold rinse to keep them from clumping

In a large pot, melt the butter and add your flour. Whisk constantly over medium-low heat for 5 minutes. It will brown a little, but don't let it burn. Pour in your milk and whisk until smooth. Cook for another 5 minutes until it gets really thick, then reduce the heat to low.

Take 1/4 cup of your sauce and slowly pour it into a cup holding your beaten egg, whisking constantly to avoid cooking the egg. Keep whisking till smooth.

Pour egg mixture back into sauce, still whisking constantly. Add in your cheese and stir to melt.

Add salt, cayenne, and pepper. Taste sauce and add more salt as needed. Pour in drained, cooked macaroni and stir until it all comes together.

Pour the whole thing into a buttered baking dish, top with some extra cheese, sprinkle with paprika and bake for 20 to 25 minutes until bubbly and golden on top.

3 PEPPER/3 BEAN CHILI

- 1 lb ground beef
- 1 tbsp olive oil
- 1 large onion (diced)
- 3 poblano peppers
- 2 red bell peppers
- 2 jalapeño pepper (seeded)
- 3 cloves garlic (minced)
- salt + freshly ground black pepper
- 2 tbsp chili powder
- 1 tsp smoked paprika
- 1 tsp ground cumin
- 1 tsp ground coriander
- 1 tsp cayenne pepper
- 1 12 oz. can/bottle lager beer
- 1 can each black beans, kidney beans, and pinto beans (drained and rinsed)
- 2 cans chopped tomatoes
- 1 can tomato paste

The Madness

In your largest pot heat your olive oil over medium-high heat. Add your onions and diced peppers. Stir until caramelized, about 5 minutes. Add your garlic and stir for an extra minute.

Add your beef to the pot and keep breaking up the clumps with your spoon as the beef cooks through (say 8 minutes or so).

Add your spices, salt, and pepper and stir until the beef and peppers are evenly coated. Then dump in your beer.

When the beer stops foaming stir in your tomato paste. Add your cans of beans and tomatoes.

Let the whole thing simmer for a while while you get your garnishes together. Add more seasonings to taste. It's great to let it cook for a while so if you make it early put it in a slow-cooker all day.

"ANN'S FAMOUS" BEAN DIP

This is a recipe my Mama got it from someone named Ann, but I've always preferred my mom's version. It's not my normal made-from-scratch kind of thing, but for a Superbowl party it's just right.

- 8 oz. package cream cheese
- 8 oz. carton sour cream
- 1 can refried beans
- 1 package taco seasoning mix
- cheddar cheese

The Madness

Mix everything all together, put it into a casserole dish, and top with grated cheddar.

Bake in 350° oven for 1 hour. (Caution: this really puffs up so don't fill dish to the top!)

My Favorite Chili Garnishes

Fresh cilantro • Sour cream or strained plain yogurt • Diced avocado • Cheddar cheese • Diced red onion

Potluck Grocery Night

I am not a foodie among foodies. Quite the opposite, in fact; I may be the only one of my friends who is passionate about the flavors, smells, textures and ambrosia of food. I once went through a phase where I came home from work and set a loaf of bread to rise every day before I even changed into more comfortable clothes. The roommate that lived with me through that period famously informed me that no matter what I made for her, it would never taste as good as Chicken A'La King from a can. Needless to say, I never cooked for her again. Our friendship remarkably remained intact.

Rather than being a small mecca for food lovers, my house has become a safe haven for my bachelor friends seeking home-cooked meals. It's not all bad; they know having to wash the dishes is a part of the deal, but they don't exactly inspire me to start experimenting with soufflés. Really, I can't complain – because my boys helped make a great success out of my favorite dinner party: Potluck Grocery Night.

As a freelancer, I'm not always in a position to host elaborate dinner parties. Over a past winter my ability to make dinner for all the friends that would show up became challenged. My being one of their only regular sources for home-cooked meals, my guys rose to the defense of their stomachs. Each of them was given a list of groceries to bring and I would do the cooking. It seemed simple enough, but I never expected the elaborate sucess it turned out to be.

As it turns out, most of my guys would have been happy to pay for my dinner had we gone out to eat. So - as none of them actually knew how to grocery shop effectively - they ended up spending the equivalent amounts for dinner for two at the grocery store. At the time I couldn't afford more groceries until my next paycheck, but for our first Potluck Grocery Night I served lamb loins with a red wine sauce and roasted asparagus. Even as the guys were doing the dishes they were asking if I would cook for them the next day if they showed up with groceries. Talk about a win-win. It became a weekly event for our group and for the next year even larger dinner parties carried the shared burden of buying the food. Recession-proofing the dinner party saved my kitchen habit and created a new circle of friends who I'll keep for life.

Rules for a successful Potluck Grocery Night

1. Assign each guest a category of food and rotate responsibilities each week

For example, one person will bring the meat ($$),
another the vegetables/sides ($),
another the beer/wine ($$), etc.
Make sure everyone takes a turn at buying the more expensive items.

2. Be specific with your grocery list

I've ended up with lime cactus beer at an Italian dinner party – don't let this happen to you.

3. Plan meals that don't take long to cook

Inevitably the person with the most key ingredient will show up last and everyone will eat late
so think 30-minute meals and you're golden.

4. Have a kitchen hang-out zone

I generally don't let people in my kitchen while I'm cooking,
but the party starts before any cooking's been done
so you need to let people hang out during the process.
Give them a safe place out of the range of hot pans of oil.

5. Don't get fancy

This is about family meals and celebrating the company – enjoy yourself and your friends.

Fried Gnocchi

16 oz. gnocchi (frozen) • 4 cups shiitake mushrooms • 4 slices thick cut bacon • 3 cups brussels sprouts • 1/4 cup pine nuts • 2 cloves garlic (minced) • 2 tbsp butter • 1 tsp olive oil • parmesan cheese

The Madness

Heat your butter in nonstick pan over medium-high heat. Add the gnocchi and cook them for 4-5 minutes, flipping them often, until browned. Set them aside in a large bowl.

Next add 1 tsp olive oil to the pan and add your mushrooms. You don't want to crowd your mushrooms in the pan, so cook them in two batches if needed. Cook them for 7 minutes, or until the mushroom liquid has cooked off. Add them to the bowl of gnocchi.

Chop your bacon and add it to the pan. When the bacon begins to crisp, add your pine nuts and brussels sprouts. Sauté 5 to 7 minutes, add your garlic, and cook an extra minute. Return mushrooms and gnocchi to pan, and sauté 2 minutes, or until warmed through.

Serve garnished with parmesan.

"The poets have been mysteriously silent on the subject of cheese."
-G.K. Chesterton

BALSAMICREDUCTIONS.COM

③

INSPIRATIONS

"Cooking is like love; it should be entered into with abandon or not at all."

— Julia Child

I love when life chooses to broaden my horizons. Maybe I've been living under a rock, but cumin hasn't been a go-to spice for me in the past. It's taken me a long time to figure out that I totally like cumin. I just hadn't used it. Just a step away from the path I've been wearing down is a new world of beautiful wonders to add to my life – all I have to do is break my routine.

BALSAMICREDUCTIONS.COM

king among the roasted vegetables

A Life-Changing Moment

Garam Masala Cauliflower

BALSAMICREDUCTIONS.COM

I believe in culinary life-changing moments. In fact, I refer to them all the time. It's not about the best thing a chef ever created for you or the five-star dining fancy dinners (though I'm up for those kind of experiences anytime they want to present themselves). My life-changing moments are quieter and more unexpected. It's the moment when I taste something new and it causes a lightning bolt explosion in my head of new ideas and revelations. Inspiring me to expand my comfort zone, they remind me to revisit forgotten ingredients and change what I stock in my fridge and pantry. They are often humble, unassuming meals, but they remind me that there is a huge world out there to explore that I haven't seen or tasted yet. They can be the most important food moments we ever have, because they actually expand the horizons of our life.

I can't really remember anymore when I discovered Indian masala. I spent a month traveling in India a few years ago and they had it as a Pringles flavor, but I'm pretty sure I was eating chicken tikka masala in Indian restaurants long before that.

It turns out there are many, many, many spice blends in India called masalas (if you have ever been there you will not find this surprising) and, though they have some general characteristics in common, recipes vary by region and none is considered more authentic than another (again – if you have ever been to India you will not find this surprising). Garam masala is generally made from peppercorns, cloves, mace, cumin, cinnamon, cardamom, nutmeg, star anise, and coriander seeds. The list goes on… regardless of the recipe it's pretty addictive stuff.

Masala dishes tend to look reddish in color, and there's a reason chicken tikka masala is the most popular dish in Indian restaurants here in the States. Tikka malasa is like the Indian version of southern BBQ. It has a lovely smokey flavor and a warm blend of aromatics that absorb deep into foods.

I picked up a garam masala on a meandering quest to make my pantry more exciting a few years ago.

I had no idea at the time that there are many masalas and I expected it to be just like tikka masala. It was a fated mistake. Knowing little to nothing of traditional Indian cooking I am pressed to make up my own recipes. I open the bag and take a big whiff of the fragrances filling my kitchen. It was sweet with cinnamon, nutmeg and cloves, complimented with a bit of heat from several kinds of pepper, and underscored with star anise. I wanted to make gingersnaps.

I have never made a dish so randomly, so instinctively and so successfully. I had never made cauliflower as an adult. I never liked it as a kid, but I was in a roasted veggie phase and thought it might do well cooked that way. Cutting it into manageable pieces is the hardest part. I didn't overanalyze it. I just drizzled the cauliflower with olive oil, cracked some fresh pepper and salt over it and started sprinkling it liberally with my new spice blend. It must have been the memory of cookies still wafting through my kitchen pushing me to do it, but I sprinkled the whole thing with a little bit of sugar for a better caramelization.

Roasting my cauliflower with garam masala was a life-changing meal. It didn't set out to be. It never appeared destined for any more greatness than a simple side dish, but it changed my life. From the very first bite, for all its simplicity, it is the single best recipe I have ever created. I can eat a full head of cauliflower in one sitting now. I need to buy masses of cauliflower if I'm willing to share this meal with anyone else.

I moved to NYC since I first created this recipe, and with every move comes a new culture to be surrounded by and new patterns and lifestyles to adjust to. I realize I haven't made this recipe in over a year. In fact I still haven't taken the time to figure out my best roasting methods for my new (very old) oven, but I do have whole cardamom on my spice rack now. I find it wildly inspiring, and I don't think that would have ever happened without my life-changing cauliflower.

My Life in a Pie

"One of the very nicest things about life is the way we must regularly stop whatever it is we are doing and devote our attention to eating."

– Luciano Pavarotti

BALSAMICREDUCTIONS.COM

Thoughts on Pie

> What does it taste like to be unemployed, starting a new job, or desperately searching to make a home?

Sometimes I just get antsy. Sometimes I just need to cook a special occasion dish without having the occasion (because I might not actually have anyone to feed it to). This year has been like that a lot. I have been spending the better part of this week looking for a job – and the rest of it cooking elaborately to ease the stir-craziness.

Beautiful in its simplicity. Literally a handful of ingredients cocooned in a piecrust nestled together in the oven. The Gorgonzola melting its way through every layer and still having enough pockets of creaminess to ooze.

This is the recipe of my life. My life is not a pie as much as a rustic tart, a little bit messy and definitely not put together around the edges. I spent my childhood up an apple tree. The only way they could get me to not pick the flowers from the tree was the promise that those flowers would lead to fruit.

My family has gone through a lot of hard times over the years and, to be honest, my life has been more savory than sweet. In the past two years I've moved to a new city and had to keep two jobs at times just to keep my head above water, but hard times don't sour life; they build us up, they make us stronger, and in the end they bring the zest and spice to the story we live. Even when there are moments of tartness there is always something sweet to smile about.

I've been self-employed for a decade as a creative professional. It has not been an easy path, but my dreams have always been worth craving. So I pile all kinds of flavors from my life into that crust that might not seem at first like they would work in a pie – fresh herbs, blue cheese, pistachios, and nutmeg… I always have faith that even if a recipe gets really out of hand there is still a creative way to bring it back together.

A little bit of this and a little bit of that, every bite different than the last, my life has never been boring. There are definitely some nuts in there. I've been pursuing the life I've always dreamed of. This past year hasn't always been pretty, but it's been flavorful, satisfying, and at the end of things it's definitely been worth repeating.

BALSAMICREDUCTIONS.COM

SAVORY APPLE TART

Dough for a single butter pie crust

1/2 cup pistachios (chopped)

1/2 cup crumbled gorgonzola cheese

1+ tbsp fresh thyme

1 1/2 tbsp honey

2 large granny smith apples (peeled and chopped)

1 tsp lemon juice

1 tsp lemon zest

Freshly grated nutmeg

¼ tsp each salt + pepper

The Madness

Toss together everything but the pastry dough in a medium sized bowl. Cover the mixture with plastic wrap while you prepare the crust.

Roll out your dough in a circle and place it on a rimmed baking sheet (in case the whole thing leaks during baking). Mound the filling in the middle of your crust and start spreading it out evenly to 1 ½" from the edge. Fold the edges of the dough over the filling.

Bake at 350° for 45 minutes to an hour until the crust is nicely browned. If it looks like the pistachios are getting too toasted you can put foil over the center.

Remove from oven and let cool at least 10 minutes before serving. Finish with a balsamic reduction drizzled over each piece.

Inventing –
are you willing to fail?

"The only real stumbling block is fear of failure. In cooking you've got to have a what-the-hell attitude."
— Julia Child

BALSAMICREDUCTIONS.COM

I was once told that I need to be more inventive by a 10 year-old boy covered in a melting gray blob that in a past life had been chocolate, mango, and neon-blue cotton candy flavored ice creams. I invent recipes all the time. I'm inventive. Or so I thought. His goatee of smeared sugary cream suited the wise smile he gave me when he explained that I was wrong. I think about things, he explained to me, and if they work in my head I do them. I need to try things that might not work. To be inventive I needed to be willing to try something that might just fail.

Am I really willing to try something that might fail? I always admire chefs who open my eyes to a new flavor combination or idea, but am I really someone who could join their ranks? I mean what kind of chef thinks of things like putting dark cherry cotton candy over seared foie gras? I don't know what it takes to have that kind of thinking, but chef Chris Lee blew my mind when he served it to me. Could I really move beyond what makes sense in my head? I don't know if I'm ready for that.

When I make something new I generally do research. I'll go to a favorite site and start plugging ingredients or similar recipes into the search function. I mostly look for things like cooking times and oven temps. I always find a logic to why I do what I do. If you put ketchup on french fries then maybe tomatoes could go well in this potato dish… It's never truly inventive. Maybe that's enough.

At brunch I was once served a cinnamon roll with bacon in it. Now I can no longer see why we all haven't been putting bacon in our sweet rolls all along. Bacon goes beautifully with maple syrup. It's only a short jump from there to cinnamon rolls through the logic of breakfast. It might not be 10 year-old approved invention, but it was a life-changing moment of its own.

Does messing up trying to recreate them count as inventive? In my heart I know it doesn't, but sometimes that's as close to failure as I'm ready to experiment with. I added red peppers to my cinnamon rolls too. Still not quite pushing that envelope of failure, red peppers have a lovely sweet flavor when cooked that makes perfect sense with bacon. Logic still killing pure creativity.

I caramelized sugar into my bacon-pepper mix. That was where things started to go wrong. Instead of blending with the cinnamon layer they spilled out like inverted caramel volcanoes destroying any baking pan sad enough to be supporting them. Their bottoms literally soaked in burnt caramel.

My 10 year-old added gummie bears to his ice cream experiment. They froze and didn't stay gummy. He considered that the only failure of his vomit-colored concoction. I added bell peppers and bacon to cinnamon rolls. I think my only problem was from sugar. Maybe we're not so different. Maybe he won't see my creations as inventive because I see the logic connecting the steps of my inspirations. Then again if I was 10 I probably wouldn't have bothered thinking through all that. I would just add chocolate to my chili because it was there to try.

BALSAMICREDUCTIONS.COM

HOW TO safely CUT AN ONION

My biggest kitchen pet peeve — the improper use of a knife. In an effort to save some fingers, let us consider the onion as a perfect knife lesson. Why an onion? Well...

ONIONS ARE QUITE ROUND

and therefore very hard to cut. Oh the dangerous ways people cut potatoes!

ONIONS WILL MAKE YOU CRY

and therefore very frustrating to chop. There are only so many tears I am willing to shed...

ONIONS ARE CRAZY DELICIOUS

and therefore need to be chopped up all the freakin' time. What dish doesn't need an onion?

so how does one deal with this beast of tears?

CHOOSE YOUR WEAPON

You need to always, always use a sharp knife. Most people's fear drives them towards the smallest, dullest knife they can find. Those knives may be less intimidating but are in fact more dangerous. Get used to using a sharp knives and your vegetable chopping will become a thousand times easier.

When it comes to knife safety, size does matter. Your knife should be large enough to halve your onion in one smooth motion. Use anything smaller and you might as well be whittling your vegetables.

DESIGN BY: CAROLYN EDGECOMB

PLAN YOUR ATTACK

EFFICIENCY IS IMPORTANT

when dealing with things that make you cry. Here is my strategy for getting perfectly diced onions with minimal tears

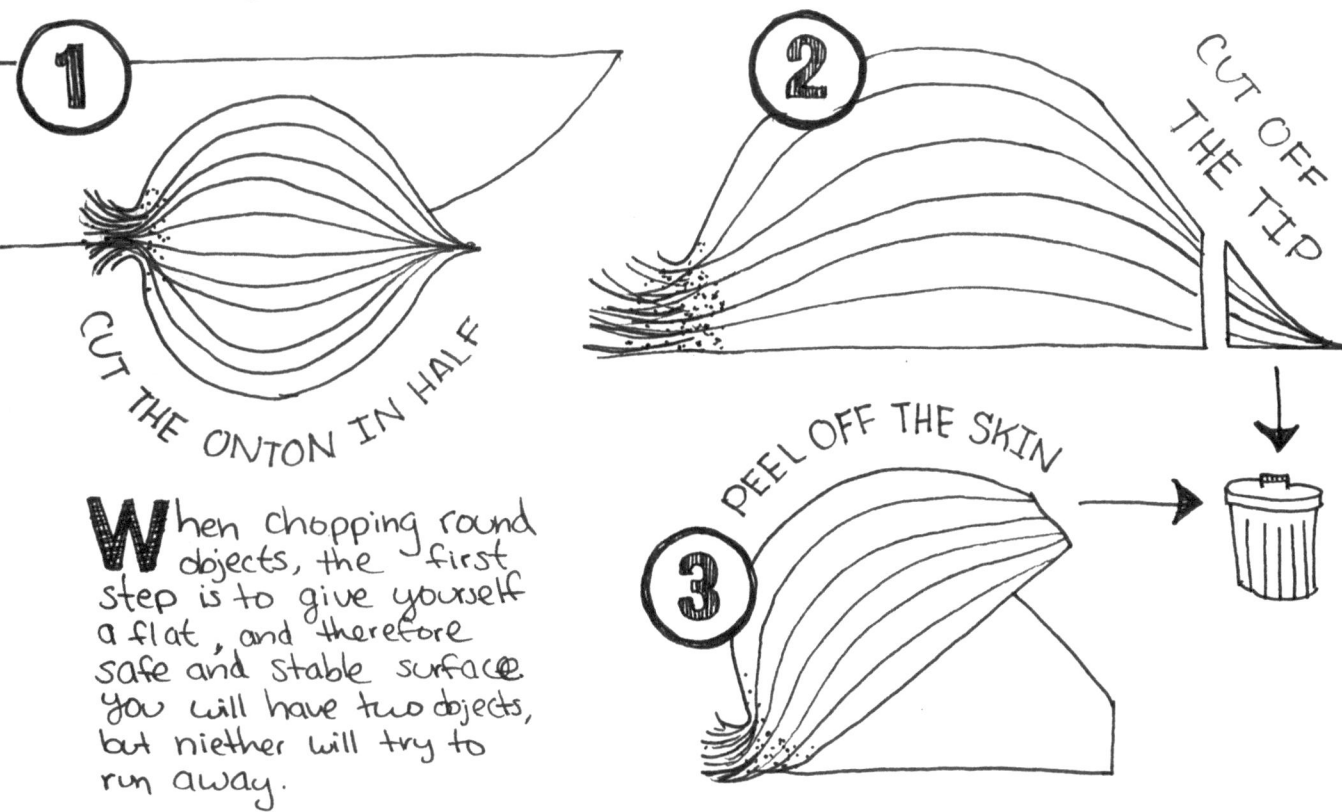

1 CUT THE ONION IN HALF

2 CUT OFF THE TIP

3 PEEL OFF THE SKIN

When chopping round objects, the first step is to give yourself a flat, and therefore safe and stable surface. You will have two objects, but niether will try to run away.

You should have two beautiful pearls of deliciousness — but they will still make you cry more than the first time you saw Titanic if you aren't careful. Don't fear, delicacy and economy will get you through.

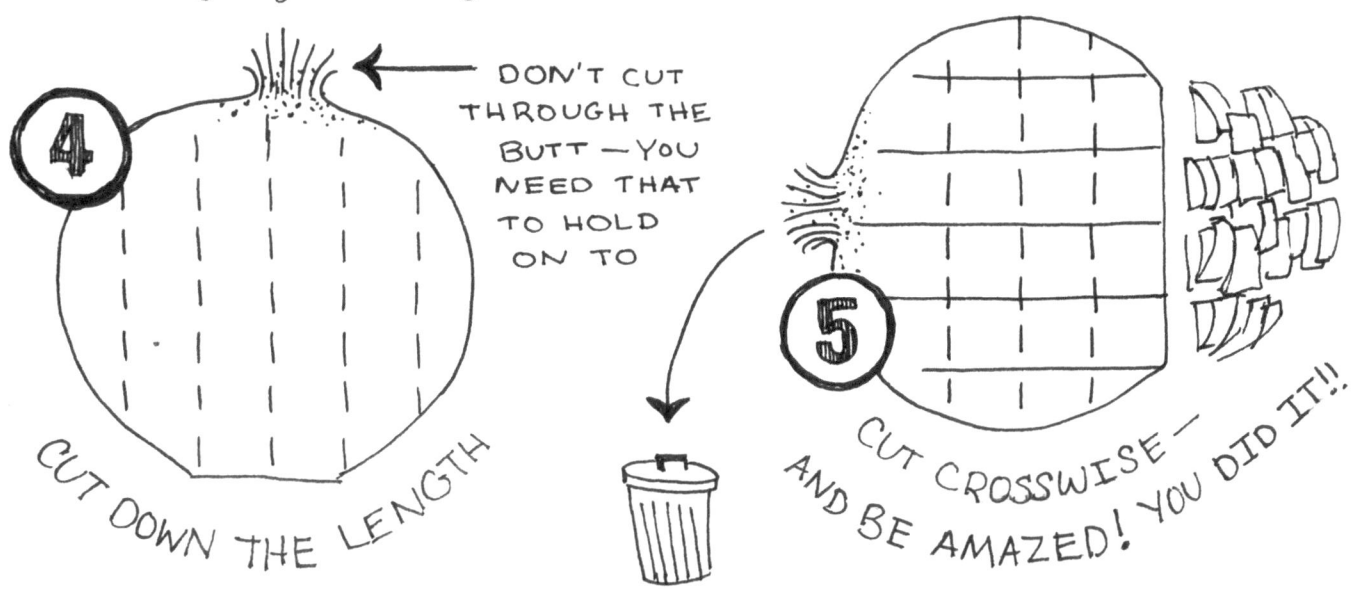

4 CUT DOWN THE LENGTH — DON'T CUT THROUGH THE BUTT — YOU NEED THAT TO HOLD ON TO

5 CUT CROSSWISE — AND BE AMAZED! YOU DID IT!!

BALSAMICREDUCTIONS.COM

4

OVER FLOW

"A good meal ought to begin with hunger."
—French proverb

"If more of us valued food and cheer and song above hoarded gold, it would be a merrier world."
—J. R. R. Tolkien

My mom has a garden and no matter how well she plans there's always a time of year where her kitchen is filled with the overflow. When you have too much of something you need to get creative. What do you do with the leftover fresh herbs starting to wilt in your fridge? There will always be room for more tomato recipes in our family. And I hope always room for more creative ideas in yours.

BALSAMICREDUCTIONS.COM

What do you do with that overflow of summer produce? Whether you're a part of a CSA, have a garden, or have a friend with a green thumb, too much produce can be a problem. From tomatoes to wilting herbs and saved leftovers, if you have a plan and some go-to recipes in your book you can keep the bounty from overwhelming your kitchen.

[Photos of Jonathan DeRaymond's Organic Farm]

BALSAMICREDUCTIONS.COM

This salad is amazing on its own, but on top of butter-fried or grilled bread it will make a meal of itself as bruschetta.

Tomato Salad

The Method

6 medium sized tomatoes (sliced or diced) • 1 large garlic clove (minced) • 1 tsp fresh basil leaves • 1/4 tsp each dried oregano, rosemary, & thyme • 1/4 tsp good salt • freshly ground pepper • 2 tbsp red wine vinegar • 2 tbsp olive oil

The Madness

Put your sliced tomatoes in a large tupperware. Blend remaining ingredients into a marinade and pour evenly over the tomatoes. Cover and refridgerate for at least 4 hours or overnight.

HOMEMADE ROASTED TOMATO KETCHUP

- 8 large tomatoes
- 1 can chopped tomatoes
- fresh basil
- fresh oregano
- olive oil
- 1/4 cup white wine vinegar
- 1/8 cup light brown sugar
- 1 tsp mustard powder
- 1 tsp cumin
- sea salt + pepper

The Madness

Cut your large tomatoes in half and arrange cut side up on a cookie sheet. Drizzle with olive oil and crack fresh pepper and sea salt over them. Roast them in 425° oven for 30-40 minutes until soft and cooked.

After your tomatoes are roasted combine all your ingredients in a large heavy pot over medium heat until it comes to a boil. Lower the heat and let the whole thing simmer uncovered for an hour. Stir occasionally to keep bits from sticking to the bottom of the pan. As it cooks keep smashing the tomatoes.

It will reduce almost in half, but this will still make a lot of ketchup. If you can it properly in sterilized jars it will keep for a long time. I didn't purée and strain my first batch, but afterwards I wish I had.

AUNT CONNIE'S BROCCOLI SOUP

My mom saves all her broccoli ends and freezes them until she has enough for this soup. I don't have that kind of patience.

- 1 bag frozen broccoli
- 1 medium onion (chopped)
- 3 cloves garlic
- 1 tsp butter
- 1 can good low-sodium chicken broth
- salt & pepper
- parmesan cheese (for serving)

The Madness

Brown the onion in butter over medium-high heat, adding the garlic to the pan just as the onion begins to brown. When garlic becomes fragrant add your broccoli and chicken broth. Cook until broccoli is soft.

I have an immersion blender, but if you don't carefully ladle the hot soup into your food processor or blender and purée. Be careful and do it in batches as necessary. It will be hot.

NYC "GRILLED" SALAD

You can't grill in NYC without being randomly blessed with a balcony or yard so we improvise.

- 1 large eggplant
- 2 zucchini
- 2 yellow squash
- 1 red onion (sliced in rings)
- 2 red bell peppers
- olive oil (for drizzling)
- sea salt, garlic powder + pepper
- 1 cup balsamic vinegar

The Madness

Preheat broiler on high. Slice your eggplant into 1" thick slices. Brush each side with olive oil and sprinkle with sea salt, garlic powder and pepper. Broil until you start to get black spots on otherwise golden sides, about 4 minutes a side. Transfer to paper towels.

Repeat this process with 3/4" slices of zucchini and squash, 1/2" slices of onion and the bell pepper cut into strips. It will take a few turns through the oven so be prepared to take a while.

While your veggies roast reduce the vinegar over medium heat until it's a syrup. Pour your balsamic reduction over your veggies and enjoy the bounty of summer!

ROASTED TOMATO SOUP

- 5 pounds ripe tomatoes
- 3 tablespoons olive oil (split)
- 4 cloves garlic (sliced)
- 1 large onion (chopped)
- 3 cups chicken broth
- salt + pepper

The Madness

Preheat your broiler on high.

Cut your tomatoes in half and scoop out the seeds. Brush each half with olive oil and stuff about half of the garlic slices into the tomatoes. Lay them out cut side up on a cookie sheet and broil them until you get some blackening.

Put your remaining olive oil in a large pot over medium-high heat and add your onion to the hot oil. Cook your onions until they become translucent and then add in the rest of your garlic slices. Cook an extra minute.

Add your tomatoes to the pot and cover the whole thing with the chicken broth. Turn your heat down to medium-low and let the pot simmer until it's hot all the way through. Salt + pepper to taste.

I use an immersion blender to make my soup puréed, but if you don't have one carefully ladel it into a blender in batches until you have a smooth soup.

Homemade roasted tomato ketchup
(see recipe on previous page)

Oven roasting tomatoes bring a lot of variety to your pantry

BALSAMICREDUCTIONS.COM

My Current Obsession:
Butter
(can you blame me?)

I have recently become obsessed with making herb-infused butters. I adore cooking with fresh herbs. It was probably one of my favorite things about cooking professionally (well, that, and my heart has been changed forever after experiencing a well-stocked walk-in fridge). If I ever find myself feeling uninspired to cook – I just pick up a couple of fresh herbs and settle happily into a tirade of ideas for what to make out of the remainders in my kitchen.

It started out innocently enough. I had fresh rosemary, Italian parsley and thyme left over from a lamb roast adventure I had set out on. So there I was with my glass of watered herbs sitting in my fridge starting to look like they'd lost the energy to hold their heads up, and I have too many leftovers in the house to justify doing anything with these poor tired friends. This is where my journey started. I had no idea that it would lead me down a path of butter-induced swooning, but this path would soon overtake the olive oil in my cooking and bring butter back as king.

Sometimes ideas are more your brain reminding you of things you already know but have yet to really explore. After reading a side note in one of my Sunset recipe annuals I had recently made a batch of citrus sugar* (it blows cinnamon out of the water as a topping for French toast). With that sitting in the back of my brain, it wasn't too far a reach to get to making an herb butter. So I pull the tiny leaves from my thyme with therapeutic meticulousness, chop it in with my rosemary and parsley, and zested in a lemon that was also waiting for the last leg of it's life to dry up.

Though I would consider my first herb butter relatively elaborate if you were setting out to make it without having a wilting cornucopia of flavorings in your kitchen, one of my favorite things about it is its casserole-ness. I just dump whatever I have available into a pound of softened butter and store it in my freezer. I even made a butter to baste my Thanksgiving turkey with in October (orange/lemon/tarragon/sage) – I can't wait. Now I eat toast with a frightening regularity and can't leave the grocery store without a fresh baguette. Before the groceries are even put away I've torn off an end of the bread so I can smother it in my new butters.

*lemon and orange zested into sugar and left to cure together

"I feel a recipe is only a theme, which an intelligent cook can play each time with a variation."
 -Madam Benoit

BALSAMICREDUCTIONS.COM

Herbs

JALAPEÑO PESTO

- 3 cloves garlic
- 1/2 cup parmesan
- 2 tbsp pine nuts
- 1/2 cup pistachios
- 3/4 cup fresh cilantro
- 3-4 jalapeños (roasted & seeded)
- 1/8 cup lime juice
- 1/2 tsp salt
- 1/2 cup vegetable oil

MIXED HERB PESTO

- 1 1/2 cups fresh herbs (basil, thyme, rosemary, parsley...)
- 1/2 tsp salt
- freshly ground pepper
- 1/4 cup good parmesan
- 2 tbsp toasted pine nuts (or walnuts)
- 2-3 cloves garlic
- 1/2 cup extra virgin olive oil

Put everything but your oil into a blender and blend until combined. Slowly drizzle your oil in while the blender is still running until everything comes together.

This pesto has enough flavor to stand up well with whole wheat pastas as well as a great topping on grilled chicken. For a gluten-free option try it over polenta or corn pasta.

Pesto keeps well in the fridge in an airtight container. Make sure to cover your pesto with a layer of oil if you plan on holding it for a while. This will preserve the bright color. My mom puts it in an ice cube tray and freezes it. Then you will have it ready for a fast meal in minutes!

Hints for Herb-Infused Butters

No recipe needed, just soften a stick of butter and add whatever chopped herbs you have to use up. You'll never want plain butter for your toast again.

- Try orange or lemon zest butters for sweeter uses like on French toast.

- Citrus zest, sage and garlic make a great rub for under the skin of your roast turkey or chicken.

- Slow cooked garlic makes an amazingly versitile infusion.

I am addicted to having fresh herbs in my kitchen, but without a garden to grow them in they are a bit of a ticking time-bomb as soon as they leave the grocery store. Since they don't last long you need to have a game plan for leftovers, and pesto is a great way to make your fresh herbs stay fragrant long after their shelf life.

"The secret of staying young is to live honestly, eat slowly, and lie about your age."
- Lucille Ball

Greek Couscous Salad

When I see a pasta salad that is just a pile of cold spiral noodles with a few light sprinkles of bell pepper and dressing, I honestly think "Really? That's what you think a side dish looks like?" I can't help it. I didn't grow up eating pasta salad but I do have some very strongly-held philosophies on pasta.

First of all, a cold pasta salad is great for the same reasons all other salads are great: freshness + color + contrasting textures and flavors. I really believe that that little bite of bell pepper tucked into your pasta salad deserves more credit for how much it gives towards the success of the group. In fact, I believe that all the little chunks of "other" deserve more attention. Chunky is good, my friends - when it comes to pasta, chunky is very good.

For any pasta salad recipe I'm generally prepared to double the amount of veggies and extras that is called for. More tomatoes! More onion! More peppers and herbs! I pile the stuff in there with great abandon. I can get to a 50:50 ratio of pasta to other and still not reach the tipping point where it becomes a salad that happens to have pasta in it.

I love Israeli couscous. It's the big pearls rather than the tiny granules. I think the texture is amazing and it stands up to more chunky recipes. The best part of couscous in the summer – it's practically a no-cook recipe. You only have to turn the stove on long enough to boil water in a kettle. Once you pour the boiling water over your couscous you leave it covered for 8-10 minutes and you're done. It's really that simple.

So this is what I call a pasta salad. You still get all the satisfaction from the pasta's comfort, but you've packed it with flavor and textures and so many good-for-you ingredients. This dish is a balance of flavors with a little bit of everything in each bite.

This is my new instant classic favorite recipe. I am adding it to my recipe rotation after only one try and that almost never happens.

GREEK COUSCOUS SALAD

- 1 cup Israeli (or large pearl) couscous
- 1 1/4 cup boiling water
- 3 tsp olive oil (split)
- Flat leaf parsley
- 1 lg cucumber (peeled and seeded)
- 1 tomato
- 1 red bell pepper
- 1 small red onion
- 1 can chickpeas (drained and rinsed)
- 4-6 oz feta cheese
- 2 lemons (zest and juice)
- 2 tbsp white balsamic vinegar
- salt + pepper

The Madness

Put your couscous into a medium heatproof bowl and add 1 tsp olive oil, stirring to coat. Then pour the boiling water (and make sure it's really boiling hot) over the couscous and cover with foil. Let that sit for 8-10 minutes until cooked to al dente. Uncover, fluff with a spoon and let cool to room temperature.

Meanwhile, dice your cucumber, bell pepper and tomato to a nice small dice – small enough to fit several flavors into one spoonful, but not so small that they can't compete with your chickpeas. Put all your veggies into a large bowl and add your chickpeas and feta. Add a liberal amount of chopped parsley, salt and pepper. Zest both lemons completely and add the zest and juice of both to the mix with the balsamic and the rest of the olive oil. Mix in your cooled couscous.

Let the whole thing rest in the fridge for a bit (no more than 3-4 hours) to let the flavors blend. Trust me it's worth it. I know that bite you already stole was great – but this thing gets amazing! Let it inspire your other pasta dishes to be chunky.

For this Meyer Lemon Tart recipe you just might have to start following online at www.balsamicreductions.com

5

SWEETS

"Life is uncertain. Eat dessert first."

-Ernestine Ulmer

"All I really need is love, but a little chocolate now and then doesn't hurt!"

-Charles M. Schulz

We all need a little sweet side of life from time to time. This summer I went through a crazy baking phase and made a lot of new discoveries. I still managed to put almond flour in almost every recipe, but if you join me in my almond fan-club then you just might find these recipes a path to your own sweet afternoon.

ORANGE INFUSED BROWNIES

- 6 oz semi-sweet chocolate chips
- 2 tbsp butter
- 1 cup flour
- 1/4 cup unsweetened cocoa powder
- 1/4 tsp salt
- 1/4 tsp baking soda
- 1/4 cup candied orange peel (chopped)
- 4 eggs
- 1 cup packed dark brown sugar
- 1/2 cup plain low-fat yogurt
- 1/4 cup canola oil
- 2 tsp orange liqueur

The Madness

Preheat your oven to 350°. Butter 6 medium ramekins and set them aside.

Melt your chocolate chips and butter in a glass bowl over a pan of lightly simmering water, stirring occasionally; don't let the water touch the bottom of the bowl.

Mix your flour, cocoa, salt, baking soda, and orange peels in a medium bowl. In a second bowl, beat the eggs and brown sugar until blended, then add your yogurt, oil and liqueur and combine. Add your melted chocolate until the whole thing comes together. Add your dry ingredients and mix until it's just moist.

Spoon your batter into your ramekins and bake for 12 to 18 minutes. I like the toothpick test - inserted in the center of your brownie it should come out just a bit fudgy. Cool completely before serving.

Sometimes You Need Something Fancy: candied orange peels

I am not one of those people who shies away from extraordinary ingredients. I mean, I'm not going to go buying a Berkshire pig leg without knowing I have a seriously great occasion for one, but this week everyday I needed a nap. I felt drained and unfocused. So I set about making something elaborate just because, just to pamper myself.

I went to visit my friend Carolyn once and she was casually making candied orange peels like it was the most natural thing in the world to be doing. I, of course, thought she was extravagantly crazy. I've never felt the need to make my own. It seemed an overly fussy thing to make. After Carolyn burned her first batch to utter black tar (I guess friends can be distracting), we went to the store for more oranges. Not only was she crazy enough to make candied orange peels, but she was willing to make them again immediately. I was intrigued. Apparently she has a cake recipe that makes all this worth it.

Sitting at her table helping her remove any signs of pith from the peels, I was beginning to see the attraction to this recipe. It's like knitting, something simple that keeps your hands busy enough to slow your mind and clear your head. This is probably the only reason that, months later, the idea of making candied orange peels stuck with me. It has my required elements of being both cheap (therefore not a tragedy if it goes awry) and something I can keep around to use later in different experiments. It also has a real element of being methodically relaxing to make and indulgent to have around.

I had never boiled things in simple syrup until they transformed. That's really all it is to candy something like this. It has all the complexity of caramel with just 3 ingredients. In the last minute there's about 30 seconds between perfectly done and starting to burn, but as I succeeded in grabbing it off the stove in time I can't imagine it's that hard to time. I only burned my fingers once on the caramel coating in setting them to cool.

They look like glowing strips of sunshine. Almost worth making just for how pretty they are. Still not sure what to do with them. They held onto that bite of citrus oil without becoming overly sweet, great to infuse into baked goods.

The City's Great Street Stalls

the making of an apricot upside-down cake

BALSAMICREDUCTIONS.COM

Every day I go for a run in the park and my run's official end is where I reach my neighborhood fruit stand guy. He's like the thrift store of grocery shopping. With only a couple of bucks in my pocket I can buy my fruit one baking adventure at a time and am never short of inspiration from the mangoes, plums, and apples sitting on boxes under his large beach umbrella. It's become how I keep track of what's in season. When apricots showed up out of nowhere at 4 for $1, I paid attention.

Apricots remind me of home and growing up in California. I don't know that they're an especially Californian fruit, but I have rarely eaten them fresh since moving east. When they're plump and firm they have an irresistible juicy flesh and tartness that is lost in their lusciously sweet, dried counterparts. Maybe it's their short ripe season or that you have to eat them right away before they go soft, but apricots taste like the very specific few weeks of summer that they arrive in.

I started baking tarts and cakes a few weeks ago as a random distraction. Baking is therapeutic in so many ways. I just love the option to whip up something elaborate and extravagant in my life with almost no expense. Sometimes you just need to feel spoiled.

The Method

1/3 cup butter

3/4 cup packed light brown sugar

Ground cardamom (for a light sprinkle over everything)

8-10 apricots

1 cup all-purpose flour

3/4 cup almond flour

1/2 tsp baking soda

1 1/2 tsp baking powder

1/2 tsp salt

1/2 cup (1 stick) butter, softened

3/4 cup sugar

a big splash of vanilla extract

2 large eggs at room temp

3/4 cup buttermilk

The Madness

Preheat oven to 375°

Heat the butter in a seasoned cast-iron skillet (at least 2 inches deep) over medium heat until it's done foaming. Reduce heat to low/med-low and sprinkle in the brown sugar evenly over butter. Cook it for 3 minutes until a caramel starts to form. Remove the skillet from the heat and sprinkle with cardamom. Arrange apricot halves cut sides down in the pan.

Stir together your dry ingredients: flour, baking powder and soda, and salt in a small bowl.

Beat together the butter, sugar, and vanilla in a large bowl at medium speed until pale and fluffy. Beat in the eggs one at a time, then beat until mixture is creamy and doubled in volume, 2 to 3 minutes.

Add your flour mixture in batches and buttermilk in batches until just combined. Gently spoon batter over apricots and spread evenly.

Bake cake in middle of oven until golden brown and a wooden pick inserted in center comes out clean, 30 to 35 minutes.

As soon as it's out of the oven you need to turn it out onto a plate. This is where you need to be careful because everything is really hot, plus there's a gooey caramel at the bottom of your pan waiting to soak into your cake. It's not difficult – just be careful and use oven mitts! Put the plate on top of your cake and with both hands flip the whole thing over. Lift off the skillet right away and let all the caramel drool out into your cake. Let it cool some before diving in, but it's amazing served warm.

BALSAMICREDUCTIONS.COM

Reasons for Cravings

I've been looking for a reason for my sudden otherwise inexplicable foray into baking so many cakes and pies this season. I had thought it was just the inspiring selections from my always-pushing neighborhood fruit stand guys. These plums were irresistible with their freckles looking like a map of the universe on their glowing purple skin… but that doesn't really explain it.

As I stand by my counter cutting through my bounty I begin feeling the comfort of the process and the excitement of seeing plums at my favorite moment of ripeness, just before they are fully sweet, still clinging to the last breaths of a tartness that's more than skin deep. I could have almost just stood there and ate through the bowl of them, but there are ideas of French pastries in my head so I continue slicing.

When I started this blog I never expected to have baking posts at all. I've always been more of a savory person. Sweets only ever really interest me when they have an unexpected balance of saltiness or bitterness or chilies and herbs or even rushes of tart. Sweets don't belong in a box. They should never be over done. Never taken for granted. Never commonplace. They should be surprising.

Were these plums really so inspiring? I went out just to buy a tart pan and baking beads just for this project. Could they really need so much when they're perfect eaten as they are?

I don't think I crave these tarts and cakes because I'm tired or stressed. I think I crave them because I crave the comforting adventure of making them. Standing by my counter slicing plums or mixing brandy and sugar into my almond flour mixture and smelling its potential as beautiful as raw talent, that is where I find my comfort. For me it will always be a different recipe, but that is where I come home to. Standing in front of the stove creating something new, that's where I come to find my balance.

PLUM TART

- 1 pie crust
- 1/3 cup almond flour
- 1/3 cup sugar
- 1 large egg
- 3 tbsp unsalted butter, room temperature
- 4 tsp brandy
- 5-6 plums
- apricot jelly

The Madness

Preheat oven to 375°.

I'll be honest – I just used a ready-made pie crust I had in the freezer. There are lots of good recipes out there to make even better crusts if you want to take the time. Either way pre-bake your crust covered with parchment and baking beads (or dried beans) until pale golden brown. Remove the parchment and beads (carefully – they are hot) and set your crust to the side to await its fillings.

The Good Part

Mix the egg, sugar, butter and 2 teaspoons brandy into your almond flour and pour the filling into crust. Arrange the sliced plums on top. Bake until plums are tender and filling is golden and set, about 40 minutes.

Put some apricot jelly and the rest of the brandy into a tiny sauce pot and heat until melted. Brush the fragrant deliciousness over the tart while still warm and let the whole thing cool. Enjoy!

Rosemary Dark Chocolate Olive Oil Cake

Olive oil and rosemary balancing seamlessly with dark chocolate in a moist but not too dense cake. This recipe is heavenly. I can't help but serve it warm from the oven, but it's actually supposed to get better with age. Don't feel guilty about that breakfast slice. It's what makes life worth living sometimes.

The Method

1 cup almond flour

1 1/4 cup all-purpose flour

1 1/2 tsp baking powder

1 tsp good salt

3/4 cup sugar

3 eggs

1 cup flavorful olive oil*

3/4 cup milk

a good handful of rosemary (plucked)

4-6 oz (depending on your mood) dark chocolate bar (chopped)

The Madness

Preheat your oven to 350°. Cut a round of parchment paper and line the bottom of your pan with it. Rub a thin layer of olive oil over your pan and set it aside.

First pluck your pile of rosemary sprigs and chop your chocolate bar. It's important to not use chips in this recipe - the texture just won't turn out right.

Then mix your dry ingredients into a large bowl. In another large bowl, whisk your eggs, then add your olive oil, milk and rosemary and whisk again. Fold the wet ingredients into the dry, gently mixing until they just come together. Stir in the chopped chocolate. Pour everything into your pan, spreading the batter evenly. Sprinkle the top with sugar for a crunchy finish.

Bake at about 40 minutes, until the top is golden brown and a toothpick comes out clean when poked into the center. The cake can be eaten warm or cool from the pan. If you are keeping it for later make sure to wrap it tightly in plastic wrap.

*I've noticed a dramatic difference in the smallest change in olive oil amounts. You want the cup to be just under the measuring line, not just over it. The lighter oil amount will give you a fluffier cake while the touch heavier hand will give you an über-moist denser cake that leaves oil on your plate.

MAMA'S BANANA BREAD

- 1/2 cup butter (melted)
- 3/4 cup sugar
- 2 eggs (lightly beaten)
- 3 medium bananas (1 cup mashed)
- 1 tsp baking soda
- 1/2 tsp salt
- 1 cup whole wheat flour
- 1 cup all-purpose flour
- 1/3 cup hot water
- 1/2 cup walnuts (chopped)

The Madness

Preheat your oven to 325º

Blend the sugar into the melted butter in a large bowl, then add the beaten eggs and mashed bananas, mixing until smooth.

In another bowl, sift the flour, whole wheat flour, salt and baking soda. Alternate adding the dry ingredients into the banana mixture with the water, adding flour a bit at a time while mixing and adding the water to keep it moist. Stir in your walnuts.

Spoon into a greased 9X5 loaf pan and bake 1 hour and 10 minutes.

Test with a tooth pick, when it comes out clean it is done. Let it cool in the pan.

ALMOND COOKIES

- 2 cups butter (slightly softened)
- 2 cups sugar
- 2+ cups almond flour
- 3 1/2 cups flour
- powdered sugar (for rolling)

The Madness

Cream your butter and sugar in a large bowl. Add your flours and mix until a dough forms. Shape in the palm of your hand into balls the size of a brazil nut.

Bake at 350º on a light colored cookie sheet for about 10 minutes or until the bottom of your cookies begin to turn golden. If you only have dark ones no worries – but the bottom of your cookies will get darker. Roll your hot cookies in powdered sugar and set on wax paper to cool. Store in an airtight container.

LEMON-CRANBERRY PINWHEEL COOKIES

- 3 cups all-purpose flour
- 1 tsp baking powder
- 1/4 tsp salt
- 1 cup butter (softened)
- 1 cup sugar
- 1 egg (beaten)
- 1 tbsp milk
- zest of 2 lemons
- 1 tsp almond extract
- 1/4 cup powdered sugar
- 1/4 cup dried cranberries (diced)
- 1/4 cup pecans (finely chopped)
- 1 tsp orange zest

The Madness

Mix together your flour, baking powder and salt in a bowl and set aside. Then beat your butter and sugar in a large bowl with an electric mixer until the mixture becomes pale.

Add your egg and milk, stir to combine. Turn your mixer down to a slower speed and add your flour mixture in a few batches. Cut your dough in half and add the almond extract, powdered sugar and lemon zest to one half. In the other half of the dough add your cranberries, pecans and orange zest. Wrap each dough in plastic wrap and chill for 10-20 minutes. Roll each dough out into a rectangle about ¼ inch thick and lay one on top of the other. Roll the sandwiched doughs into a log and chill for at least 2 hours.

Preheat your oven to 375º.

Unwrap the log and cut into ¼ inch slices. Put your slices on a parchment-lined cookie sheet and bake until the edges turn golden, about 12 minutes. Let them cool before storing in an airtight container.

PEPPERMINT COOKIES

- 3 cups all-purpose flour
- 1 tsp baking powder
- 1/4 tsp salt
- 1 cup butter (softened)
- 1 cup sugar
- 1 egg (beaten)
- 1 tbsp peppermint extract
- 1 cup crushed candy canes

The Madness

Mix together your dry ingredients in a bowl and set aside. Then put your butter and sugar in a large bowl and beat together with an electric mixer until it becomes pale. Add your egg, candy canes and extract, stir to combine. Turn your mixer down to a slower speed and add your flour mixture in a few batches. Lay the dough on some plastic wrap and form 2 logs of dough (you can always make 3 shorter ones if that will fit in your fridge better).

Wrap and chill for at least 2 hours.

Preheat your oven to 375º.

Unwrap the dough logs and cut into ¼ inch slices. The candy canes melt when you bake these cookies, so they don't make for the most optimal use of cookie cutters. Hearts were the best I've ever managed. Anyway, put your slices on a parchment-lined cookie sheet and bake until the edges are just tanning, about 12 minutes. Let them cool on a rack and try to keep everyone from eating them while they're resting.

The (almost) Secret Recipe of the (almost) Famous Ginger Snaps

Have you ever noticed if someone calls their dish "famous" it is inevitably a secret recipe? I don't know why this is so true but it's an easily observable phenomenon. If it were to preserve the marketability of a recipe brand that would be one thing, but typically no one has actually heard of this "famous" dish – nor is anyone trying to market it. This is the case with my mother's ginger snaps.

A holiday tradition in my family that is possibly a more important part of Christmas than gifts. These cookies deserve to be famous. They are not. Not really anyway.

We eat so many of them that my mom's only willing to make them a few times a year (and always only between November and January). She got the recipe while in college. When my mother loves something it is no small love. Her basic recipe is a double batch, and we typically double that every time, so it's a load of work to keep our house supplied. Now that we all live out on our own it's 5 times more work to keep all of our houses full for the season.

The Method

- 1 1/4 cup margarine (softened)
- 2 1/2 cups sugar ….. PLUS 1 cup to roll the dough balls in.
- 2 eggs
- 1/2 cup molasses
- 4 cups flour
- 2 teaspoons baking soda
- 2 teaspoons cinnamon
- 2 teaspoons ground ginger
- 1 teaspoon ground cloves

The Madness

Preheat your oven to 375°

Beat the butter, sugar, eggs and molasses in a large mixing bowl until smooth. In a second mixing bowl mix your baking soda and spices with your flour (I am very heavy handed with the spices).

Add the flour to wet ingredients slowly, about a cup at a time.

Roll into balls about ¾" in diameter. Roll the dough balls in the reserved sugar. Place well spaced on the cookie sheet, as they spread.

Bake until done (about 8 minutes). That is up to you, my mom likes hers almost burnt ("extra crunchy" as she calls it).

BALSAMICREDUCTIONS.COM

BALSAMICREDUCTIONS.COM

BALSAMICREDUCTIONS.COM

Thank You

This book is dedicated to my kickstarter supporters
who helped change my life.

Kirk Love	Patricia Cobb	Mark Gambol
Stephanie Ricketts	Andy Weissman	Mach & Colleen Schoneveld
Marlena Cobb	Mark & Erin Schoneveld	Adri Platner
Irene Yanko	Ayodele Yusuf	Gambitnoir
The Halko Family	Carolyn Edgecomb	Adam Spielberg
Jeremy Hindman	Sean Metzgar	Lauren & Eric Helm
Palmer Enfield	Jendra Jarnagin	Stephanie Kelley
Adriana Stimola	Cindy Phillips	Veronica Stroever
Bob Gorelick	Kurt Krukenberg	Bryan Shay
Dennis Norwood	Dave & Charisse Galliguez	Michael Naess
Jeff Bishop	Vanessa Kellogg	Stephen Hollifield
Christopher Goldsberry	Rebecca & Brandon Cheek	Barbara Anders
Amy Van Vessem	Andrew Harter	Beth Scheraga
Robert Bridgens	Bethany & John Hong	Edward J. Eberwine III
Mark Rode	Brian Devine	Milan Misko
Rebekah DeRoco	David & Molly Schoneveld	Emily Hall Smith
Emily Mangini	David Nicholas	Indira Cheruvu
Radu Tutos	Abe & Emily Loper	Rob Pierce
Ashley Frament	Amanda Leigh Cobb	J. Ennis Kirkland
Becky Armstrong	Rosie duPont	Rene Braud
Chris Kellett	Allyson Lysaght	Srikant Cheruvu
Courtney Queen	Sonny Ratcliff	Patricia Smith
Mark Filipps	Gary Radin	Shane Phillips
Leanne MacDonald	Tom Ervin	Paul Schoneveld
Chris Vasquez	Ibukun Aisha Yusuf	BKLYN Larder
Mike Petrow	Angelina Woehr	The Tea Lounge Crew

BALSAMICREDUCTIONS.COM